J   **Sutcliff, Rosemary.**
    Heather, oak, and olive; three stories. Illustrated by
Victor Ambrus. ₁1st ed.₁ New York, Dutton ₁1972₁

    120 p. illus.   22 cm. $4.95

    CONTENTS: The chief's daughter.—A circlet of oak leaves.—A
crown of wild olive.

Central

           1. Civilization, Ancient—Fiction₁   I. Ambrus,
Victor G., illus.   II. Title.   STJ 11/72

PZ7.S966He   79-133124
ISBN 0-525-31599-3   MARC

Heather, Oak, and Olive

Heather, Oak, and Olive

Three Stories by
ROSEMARY SUTCLIFF

Illustrated by Victor Ambrus

C. 4C

E. P. DUTTON & CO., INC.   NEW YORK

First published in the U.S.A. 1972 by E. P. Dutton & Co., Inc.

The Chief's Daughter text copyright © 1966 by Rosemary Sutcliff;
illustrations copyright © 1967 by Victor Ambrus

A Circlet of Oak Leaves text copyright © 1965, 1968 by Rosemary
Sutcliff; illustrations copyright © 1968 by Victor Ambrus

A Crown of Wild Olive (originally published as *The Truce of
the Games*) text copyright © 1971 by Rosemary Sutcliff; illustrations
copyright   © 1971 by Victor Ambrus

SBN: 0-525-31599-3   LCC: 70-133124

Designed by Dorothea von Elbe
Printed in the U.S.A.
Second Printing, April 1973

Contents

The Chief's Daughter

THE Dun, the Strong-Place, stood far out on the headland, seeming almost to overhang the Western Sea. Three deep turf banks ringed it round, and where the hawthorn stakes of the stockade had taken root here and there, small stunted branches with salt-burned leaves grew bent all one way by the sea wind.

The Chief's big round Hall where the Fire of the Clan never died on the hearth, stood at the highest part of the enclosure, with his byres and barns and stables, and the women's huts clumped about it. But in quiet

times only the Chief himself and his kindred and household warriors lived there, while the rest of the Clan lived in the stone and turf bothies scattered over the landward side of the headland. Only when the raiders came out of the West in their skin-covered war boats, would the whole Clan drive their cattle into the spaces between the sheltering turf banks, and take refuge in the Chief's stronghold.

It was such a time now, the whole enclosure crowded with men and women and children and dogs and lean pigs, while the cattle lowed and fidgeted uneasily in

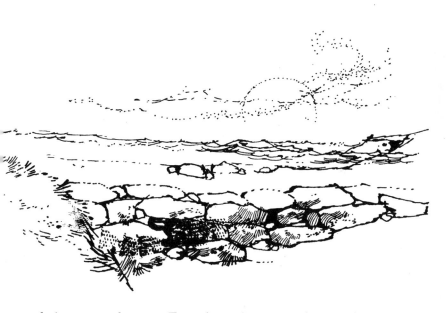

their cramped space. For, three days ago, the war boats had come again, and the Irish raiders were loose along the coast of Wales, scouring the hills for cattle and slaves.

On the sloping roof of the hut where the black herd bull lived, a boy and a girl were sprawling side by side. The boy would rather have climbed to the roof of the Hall, because from there you could get a further view to the west, but the turf of the Hall roof, tawny as a hound's coat, was growing slippery with the dryness of late summer, while the bull-house was thatched with

heather that gave you something to dig your toes and
heels into, so that you did not keep sliding off all the
time.

The girl was ten years old, dark and slight, like most
of the folk in the headland Strong-Place below her. She
had found a grey and white seagull's feather caught in
the rough thatch, and was trying to twist it into her
long dark hair. The boy, who lay propped on one elbow
staring out to sea, was older, with hair and eyes almost
the same colour as the string of amber round his neck.
He did not belong to the girl's People, but was a
prisoner in their hands, left behind wounded, the last
time the Irish war boats came.

The girl gave up trying to make the feather stay in
her hair, and sat chewing the end of it instead. "Dara,
why will you always be staring out towards the sunset?"

The boy went on staring. "I look towards my home."

"If you loved it so much, why did you leave it and
come raiding in ours?"

He shrugged. "I am a man. When the other men go
raiding, should I sit at home spinning with the women?"

"A *man!* You're only twelve, even now! Only two
years older than I am!"

That time the boy did not answer at all. The sea
creamed on the rocks under the headland, and from
beneath the heather thatch came the soft heavy puffing
of the herd bull. After a while the girl threw the feather
away, and said crossly, "All right, go on staring into
the sunset. *I* am not wanting to talk to you."

"Why should you want to talk to a prisoner?" Dara snapped, looking round at last. "You did not have to come climbing up here after me."

"You would not have been even a prisoner, if I had not pleaded for you. They meant to sacrifice you to the Black Mother; you know that, don't you?"

"I know that. You've reminded me often enough," Dara said between his teeth. "It is a great honour that Nessan the Chief's daughter should plead for me. I must remember and be grateful."

The girl seemed to have got over her sudden crossness, and looked at him consideringly. "Yes, I think you should," she said after a moment, "for besides pleading for you with Father *and* with Laethrig the Priest, I gave my best blue glass arm-ring to the Mother, that she might not be angry with us for keeping you alive!"

And then someone came past the bull-house with a clanking pail, and looked up and called to Dara that it was time he came down and took his share of the work, for the cattle needed watering.

Just below the Chief's Hall, where the land began to drop, a spring burst out from under a grey boulder. It filled a small deep pool almost like a well, then spilled over and away down the narrow gully it had worn for itself, through the gap left for it in the encircling banks, and dropped over the cliff edge making a thread of white water among the rocks, until it reached the sea. That evening it seemed to the men watering the cattle that it was running unusually low, and when the pails

7

were brought up out of the well-pool, it took longer than usual to refill. Some of them looked at each other a little anxiously. But the spring had never been known to dry up, no matter how many men and cattle drank from it. They were imagining things. It would be its usual self in the morning.

But in the morning, when it was time to water the cattle again, and the women came to draw the day's pitcher-full for their households, there was scarcely any water spilling over into the little gully at all.

"It has been a dry summer, I am thinking," one woman said.

Another shook her head. "We have had dry summers before."

"It is in my mind," said a man standing by with a pail

for his cattle, "that this thing must be told quickly to the Chief."

The Chief came, and looked into the sullen stillness of the well, and then up into the heat-milky sky, pulling the dark front-locks of hair on either side of his face as he always did when troubled. "It must surely rain soon," he said after a while. "Maybe rain is all we need. But meanwhile the cattle must be doing with half measure, and see that the women take their pitchers away only half full."

What he did not say, and no one else said either, for

even to speak of such a thing would be unlucky, was, "If the water fails, the stronghold fails also."

All that day the people went about with anxious eyes, returning again and again to look at the spring. By evening, the pool had barely filled up again, and not one drop was spilling over into the stony runnel.

Then the Chieftain sent for Laethrig the Priest. And Laethrig came, very old and brittle, like a withered leaf, in his mantle of beaver skins with his necklaces of dried seed pods and slender seabird bones rustling and rattling about his neck. And he sat down beside the spring and went away small inside himself so that looking into his eyes was like looking through the doorway of an empty hut. And it seemed a long time, to the men and women waiting about him, before he came back and looked out of his eyes again.

"What is it?" they asked, softly like a little wind through the headland grasses. "What is it, Old Wise One?"

The old man said, "It is as I feared. The Black Mother is angry with us because we did not slay in her honour the Irish captive."

The Chieftain had grown fond of the red-haired boy, and a shadow crossed his face, but he only said, "The Will of the Goddess is the Will of the Goddess. What must we do, Old Wise One?"

Laethrig the Priest got slowly to his feet, and drew his beaver-skin mantle about him. "At first dark, we must begin to cry to the Goddess, on the sacred drums, and at moon-set we must make the sacrifice. Then the Black Mother will no longer be angry with us, and she will give us back the living water, so that our spring will run full again."

Nessan, on the outskirts of the crowd, had the sudden dreadful feeling of being tangled in a bad dream. In the dream she saw Dara standing quite still in the grip of the huge warrior who had caught hold of him. He looked more bewildered than afraid, and she thought

that he had not really understood what Laethrig said. He and she could manage well enough when they talked together, but the tongue of the Irish raiders was different in many ways from the tongue that her own people spoke, and he might not have understood.

Despite the hot evening, her feet seemed to have frozen to the ground, and she could not move or make a sound; and still in the bad dream she saw them take Dara away. She knew that he had begun to be afraid now; he looked back once as though with a desperate hope that someone would help him. And then he was gone.

Nessan unfroze, and her head began to work again. It whirled with thoughts and half-ideas chasing each other round and round, while she still hovered on the edge of the murmuring crowd. And then quite suddenly, out of the chase and whirl, a plan began to come, detail after detail, until she knew exactly what she must do.

The three Drummers of the Clan stepped into the open space beside the spring, and began to make a soft eery whispering and throbbing with their finger-tips on the sacred wolfskin drums, and all the Clan who were not already there, came gathering as though at a call. The sun was down and the shadows crowding in, made sharp-edged and thin by the moon, as she slipped away unnoticed by the crowd. The rest of the Dun was almost deserted now; no one noticed her as she slipped by like another shadow. She ran to the place where the stream gully zigzagged out through its gap at the cliff's edge—

everything depended on that—then to the out-shed where tomorrow's bread was stored; then to a certain dark bothie among the sleeping-places. It was easy to find the right one, for the huge warrior who had taken Dara away stood on guard before its door-hole, leaning on his spear. Her heart was beating right up in her throat as she started to work her way round to the back of the bothie, so that she was sure only the throbbing of the drums kept the spear man from hearing it, and was terrified that they might stop.

But she reached the back of the bothie, and checked there, carefully thinking out her next move.

Many of the living huts had a loose strip of turf in the roof, which could be turned back to let in more air in hot summer weather, and by good fortune, this was one of them. She reached up (the rough stone walls were so low that the edge of the roof came down to only just above her head) and felt for the rope of twisted heather that held the loose end of the summer-strip in place, and found it. She pulled it free, but standing on the ground, she could not reach up far enough to raise the turf flap more than a few fingers' lengths. Well, that did not matter, so long as she could get a hand inside. She got a good hold on the top of the hut wall; it was easy enough to find a toe-hold in a chink between two stones, and she was a light as a cat. Next instant she was crouching belly-flat along the edge of the roof, listening for any sound from the man on the far side of the hut.

No sound came. She found the edge of the summer-

strip again, and lifted it a little and then a little more, until she could let it fold back on itself, with no more sound than a mouse might have made in the thatch.

In the pitch darkness below the square hole, she thought she heard quick breathing and then a tiny startled movement. She ducked her head and shoulders inside. "Dara! It's me—Nessan."

And Dara's voice whispered back, "Nessan!"

"Don't make a sound! There's a man with a spear outside. Have they tied you up?"

"Yes—to the house-post."

"I am coming down." Nessan felt for the right hold, and swung her legs into the hole, and dropped. Any sound that she made was covered by the wolfskin drums which woke at that moment into a coughing roar. Then she had found Dara and pulled her little food knife from her belt and was feeling for the rawhide ropes that lashed his hands behind him to the tall centre pole of the bothie.

"What does it all mean?" he whispered. "What have I done?"

"They say the Black Mother is angry, and that is why the spring is failing. They say that they must kill you at moon-set tonight, and then she will not be angry any more."

Dara gave a gasp, and jerked in his bonds.

"Hold still, or I shall cut you! But they shan't do it! I will not let them!"

"How can you stop them?" Dara's voice shook a little

in the dark. "Go away, Nessan—go away before they find you!"

Nessan didn't bother to answer that. She went on sawing at the rawhide ropes, until suddenly the last strand parted. She gave a little sound like a whimper, under her breath. "There. Now come!"

She could feel him rubbing his wrists to get the feeling back. "You first; you're lighter than me."

She did not argue. There was no time. She reached up for the rough wall top, and felt Dara heave from below. She came up through the glimmering sky-square, and went right over in a kind of swooping scramble, to land on the earth outside. There was a faint grunt and a scuffle, the dark shape of Dara's head and shoulders appeared through the hole, and next instant he had dropped on to his feet beside her.

She caught his hand, and began to run, out towards the seaward side of the Dun, away from those terrible drums. When she pulled up, panting, they were at the gap in the turf walls where the stream gully passed through.

"Look! This is the way you must go—they don't guard this side. And when you're away, you'll be able to find a war band of your own people."

They had scrambled down the dry runnel-bed, right to the far edge of the gap, and the cliff plunged almost from their feet to the sea creaming among the rocks far down below. Dara looked—and down—and down—and swallowed as though he felt sick.

"You've got to go that way!" Nessan whispered fiercely. "It's easy."

"If it's so easy, why don't they guard it?"

"Because the water from the spring makes it slippery, and no one could keep his footing on the wet rocks. But now it's dry. Don't you see? It's dry!" She fished hurriedly down the front of her tunic, and held something out to him.

"Here's a barley cake. Now go quick!"

But the boy Dara hesitated an instant longer. "Nessan, why are you doing this?"

"I—don't want you to be killed."

"I don't want to be killed either. But Nessan, what will they do to you?"

"They will not do anything. No one will know that
I had anything to do with it, if only you go quickly."

Dara tried to say something more, then flung an arm
round her neck in a small fierce hug and next instant
was creeping forward alone.

She was half crying, as he crouched and slithered
away, feeling for every hand- and foot-hold along the
grass-tufted cliff edge, and disappeared in the black
moon-shadow of the turf wall. She waited shivering,
ears on the stretch for any sound. Once she heard the
rattle of a falling pebble, but nothing more. At last she
turned back towards the Chief's Hall, and the quicken-
ing throb of the wolfskin drums.

To Dara, that time of clinging and clambering along
the shelving ledges of bare rocks and summer-burned
grass, with the turf wall rising steeply on his right side,

and on his left the empty air and the drop to the fanged rocks and the sea, was the longest that he had ever known. And at every racing heart-beat he was terrified of a false step that would send him whirling down into that dreadful emptiness with the rocks at the bottom of it, or betray him to the terrible little dark men within the Dun. But at last the space between the turf wall and cliff edge grew wider, and then wider still, and soon he was clear of the Dun, and the deserted turf huts scattered inland of it, and he gathered himself together and ran.

After a while he slowed down. No sense in simply running like a hare across country, and he had no idea in what direction he would find the war bands of his own people. And at that moment he realized that he had no weapon. Nessan had slipped her knife back into her belt after she had cut his bonds, and neither of them had thought of it again. He was alone and unarmed in an enemy country. Well, there was nothing to do but keep going and hope that he would not need to kill for

food or run into any kind of trouble before he found his own people.

Presently, well into the hills, he came upon a moorland pool, where two streamlets met. It was so small and shallow that he could have waded through it in several places, and scarcely get wet to the knee. And the moon, still high in the glimmering sky, showed him an upright black stone that stood taller than a man, exactly between the two streamlets where they emptied themselves into the pool. A black stone, in a countryside where other stones were grey; and twisted about the narrowest part near the top, a withered garland of tough moorland

flowers: ling and ragwort and white-plumed bog-grasses.

Dara stood staring at it with a feeling of awe. And as he did so, a little wind stirred the dry garland, and from something fastened among the brittle flower-heads, the moonlight struck out a tiny blaze of brilliant blue fire! Nessan's blue glass arm-ring! He caught his breath, realizing that this must be the Goddess herself, the Black Mother. But at the same instant, he noticed the spear which stood upright in the tail of the pool. A fine spear, its butt ending in a ball of enamelled bronze; an Irish spear!

His own people must have passed this way and come across the Goddess whose People they had been raiding, and left an offering to turn aside her anger. He noticed also that the spear, set up in what seemed to be the place where the two streams joined before the feet of the Black Mother, had caught a dead furze branch on its way down and twigs and birch leaves and clumps of dry grass, even the carcase of some small animal, had drifted into the furze branch and clung there, building up into something like a small beaver's dam, and blocking the stream so that it had spread out into a pool. And as the pool grew high enough, it had begun to spill over a new runnel that it was cutting for itself down the hillside.

Dara was not interested in the changed course of a stream, but he needed that spear; needed it so badly that his need was greater even than his fear of taking it.

He caught a deep breath and turned to the tall garlanded stone that seemed to him now to stand like a queen in the moonlight. "Black Mother, do not be angry. I must have the spear. See, I will leave you a barley cake and my amber necklace instead. That is two gifts for one!"

And his heart racing, he stepped into the water and pulled up the spear. For a moment he expected the sky to fall on him or the hillside to open and close again over his head. But nothing happened, and he went on his way, following the faint track of the war band that he could pick up here and there by trampled grass or a thread of dark wool caught on a bramble spray, and the droppings left by driven cattle.

And behind him, now that the spear that had held it was gone, little by little the dam washed away, and the pool sank, as the water returned to its old stream bed and sang its way downhill, to disappear under a bramble bush in the place where it had always gone underground before the raider left his spear for the Black Mother.

And where it went from there, under the turf and the rocks and the hawthorn bushes on its way to the sea, was a secret that neither Dara nor the Irish raiders nor Nessan's People knew. Only the stream singing to itself in the dark, knew that secret.

At moon-set, when the drumming grew still, and the pine knot torches all round the space below the Chief's Hall began to flare more brightly in the dark time before the dawn, several warriors of the Chief's kin went to fetch Dara from his prison. They came running back shouting that the boy was gone! The word ran like a squall of wind through the crowd, and the Chief sprang up from his seat of piled oxhides. "Gone?"

"There's not a sign of him—not a shadow."

"And his cut bonds lying beside the centre post, and the summer-strip turned back from the roof edge!"

The Chief turned upon the warrior who had guarded the door-hole. "Istoreth, what do you say as to this?"

The warrior looked his Chief steadily in the eye, but in the light of the torches his face was ashy, for he knew what to expect. "I kept my watch. I saw nothing, I heard nothing," he said.

"I'll have you kept your watch! And the Black Mother waits for her sacrifice. If the boy is not found, then you must take his place. Is it fair and just?"

"It is fair and just," the man said.

The Chief turned from him to the warriors standing close around. "Go you and search all within the stockade—every corner, every hut."

But before they could move to obey him, Nessan, on the dark fringe of the crowd, heard her own voice, high and silvery and very clear, as though it were not hers at all but somebody else's, "You will not find him! He is not here!"

There was a sudden hush, everyone looked towards her, and in the hollow heart of the hush, the Chief her father demanded in a terrible voice, "Nessan, what thing have you done?"

Nessan walked forward into the torchlight, the people parting to let her through. "I helped him to escape, my Father, through the gap where the spring water goes. It is dry, not slippery, now that the water—does not run."

The Chief groaned and covered his face with his hands, and Laethrig the Priest, who had been standing by all this while, spoke for the first time. "And you are daring to come forth here and tell us of it?"

"Yes, Old Holy One." Nessan tried desperately to steady her voice.

"You are very brave, my child, or very foolish!"

Nessan drew a long shivering breath. "You cannot kill Istoreth. It was not his fault. I—I knew when I helped Dara away, that if the well did not fill again, I must come here instead of him."

"It is of your own choosing," said the old priest, very gently. "So be it, then; come here to me."

"No!" cried the Chief.

"Yes!" said the old priest, as gently as ever. He was holding the black pottery bowl that was used for only one thing, to hold the drink that brought the Long Sleep at the time of sacrifice.

Nessan took a step towards him, and wavered for a moment, then walked steadily forward.

Everything was very quiet, nobody moved or whispered in all the crowd; the only sound was the restless stirring of the thirsty cattle. And then into the quiet, there fell a tiny sound; a soft "plop" and then a faint trickling from the well that had been sullenly silent all night long.

"No, wait!" one of the women cried.

"Listen!"

"What to, then?"

"There it is again!"

"It is the well! The spring is coming back to life!"

That time all those near enough to the spring heard it, and a great gasp went up from them. They crowded round the well-pool; then they were parting and pushing back to make a path for the Chief and Laethrig to pass through.

Nessan did not move. She stood where she was, and shut her eyes tight; she heard another plop and a wet green trickling, and the murmur of the crowd; and then her father crying out in a great triumphant voice, "The water is rising! You see, Old Holy One? You hear?"

"I see and I hear," said the old priest. "It is in my heart that the Black Mother is no longer angry with us. . . ."

And she knew from his voice that he had gone away small inside himself, so that if you looked into his eyes it would be like looking through the doorway of an empty hut.

Everyone waited, hearing the plop and ripple of the refilling well. And then at last Nessan heard the old man sigh, and the dry rustle of his necklaces, as he stirred and came back to himself. "The Black Mother has spoken to me. She calls for no more sacrifice in this

matter; she says the willingness is enough—the willingness is enough."

Nessan opened her eyes, half dazzled for the moment by the flare of the torches, and saw the Chief her father coming towards her, and flung herself into his arms, crying partly for sorrow that Dara was gone, and partly with relief so that there was not enough room for it all inside her, and partly because she was suddenly more tired than she had ever been in all her life.

And the Chief picked her up and carried her away to her own sleeping-place in the women's hut behind the great Hall. She was asleep before he laid her down on the dappled deerskin rugs.

At the same time, far up in the hills, a broken curlew's feather, the very last that was left of the dam, shook itself clear of the bog-myrtle of the stream bank, and went eddying downstream.

A Circlet of Oak Leaves

OUTSIDE, a little mean spring wind came snuffling up from the river, humming across the parade ground of the great fortress in the dark, and tumbling the garbage along the narrow streets of Isca Silurium, but within the open door of the *Rose and Wine Skin* was lamplight and the warmth of braziers, and a companionable rise and fall of voices.

Three young Auxiliary Cavalrymen stood propped against the high trestle table at the far end, talking to the retired Gaulish Javelin man who kept the place, but each with an ear twitching towards the nearest corner, where a knot of Legionaries with long-service bracelets and faces like tanned harness leather, had pulled two benches together and were setting the world to rights.

"That's what I say!" One of the veterans brought an open hand down on the bench beside him with a slam that set the wine cups jumping. "All this talk about the need for more Cavalry is so much moon's-milk. It's *us*, the line-of-battle lads that carry the day, every time."

Another nodded, consideringly. "It's the speed and mobility they're after, of course."

And a third laughed into his wine cup. "Comes in useful for retreating."

"It was just the same, that time the Picts broke through the Northern Wall—the time the Legate was killed. Six or seven wings of Cavalry, the 6th had with them, when they went up to deal with that lot of blue painted devils, and so far as I can make out the Dacians were the only ones that didn't run like redshanks at the first sound of the Pictish yell."

The young Auxiliaries had been listening to all this, staring straight before them. Now, one of them, flushing slowly crimson under his ragged cap of barley-pale hair, stepped out from the rest and edged over to the veterans.

"I ask pardon, sir," he swallowed thickly. "My mates and I couldn't help hearing. You did say, 'As far as you could make out'? You weren't there yourself, then, sir?"

The first veteran looked up, his thick brows shooting towards the roots of his hair. "No, I'd a brother there, if it concerns you. He lost a hand when the left flank was crumpled up—it helped him to remember."

"I'm sorry, sir, but that—losing a hand, I mean— mightn't help him remember very clearly."

One of the group gave a snort of laughter. "It's a Cavalry cub. You've hurt his honour, Gavrus."

"Too bad, Hirpinius," Gavrus said. "I've had enough of you, my lad. You're only a little boy, and you don't know anything yet but what the recruiting officer told

you. Everyone knows the Tungrians and the Asturians ran like redshanks. Come back and quarrel with me when you've learned to grow a beard!"

There was a roar of laughter from the rest of the Legionaries. The boy's hands clenched into large knuckled red fists. His mates had begun to come up behind him. At any moment there was going to be trouble, and the wine-shop owner looked on anxiously. He had been an Auxiliary himself, and quite clearly, whatever happened, the boys were going to get the sticky end of the vine staff.

But at that moment a rangy, loose-limbed man who had been lounging on the bench nearest the door unfurled himself lazily and came across to join the group.

"The Picts fired the heather, and the flames stampeded the horses."

Everyone turned to stare at him, including the shop's owner, who knew him well enough: head man to old Lyr the horse-breeder, who came down a couple of times a year, with wild-eyed, rough-broken three-year-olds to sell to the garrison horse-master. And the man stared back at them out of slightly widened eyes that seemed pale as rain by contrast with his dark hard-bitten face.

Out of a moment's startled silence, Gavrus said, "And who in Hades are you?"

"My name is Aracos, for what that's worth; from Thrace in the beginning, from the hills a day's trail westward now!"

34

"So. And it was fire that stampeded the horses?"

"Yes."

"You were *there*, I suppose?"

"Yes."

There was a general gasp, and somebody spluttered into his wine cup.

Then Gavrus, still only half believing, repeated, "You *were* there?"

"I've lived long enough to be other things before I was a horse-breeder."

"Tungrian Cavalry? or Asturian?"

"Dacian," Aracos said, and added obligingly, "the ones who didn't run like redshanks, you know."

Gavrus took a long swig at his wine, studying him over the rim of the cup all the while, then set it down. "Oddly enough, I believe you. Just by way of interest, why *didn't* the Dacian horses stampede with the rest?"

"Because the Dacians teach their horses tricks. Haven't you ever seen a Dacian squadron showing off? Standing on horseback or clinging under the brute's belly, or leaping them through the flames of a fire-trench? When the Picts' fire came down on us, our horses were used to the flames, and not afraid."

The young Auxiliaries looked at each other; one of them whistled under his breath.

"So simple as that, eh?" Abruptly Gavrus shifted along the bench, his leathery face breaking into a grin. "You've your cup with you—join us and fill up to show there's no ill feeling; you too, my bold infants. Hai,

35

Landlord, more wine all around!" There was a general shifting up to make room, and in a few moments, the Auxiliaries still a little stiff, they were all sitting together, while the shop's owner himself brought the wine.

Pouring the harsh red stuff into the cup Aracos held out, he said, reproachfully, "It must be four—five times you've been in here, and never said you were one of us."

"You never asked me," Aracos said.

Under the warming influence of the wine, the atmosphere were growing friendly, and Aracos felt the warmth of old comradeship and a familiar world drawing him in again, doing more, had he but realized it, than ever the rough Sabine wine could do, to make him unwary.

They talked of girls, the price of barley-beer, the evil-mindedness of Centurions, and so came back again to old battles, to the one particular battle, ten years past.

One of the Legionaries, a dark-faced man more silent than his fellows, looked up abruptly from the depth of his wine cup into which he had been staring. "Of course! *That* was it!"

"Um?" Gavrus prompted.

"There was something else about that fight—I was trying to remember what it was."

"And what was it?"

"One of the Auxiliaries earned himself the Corona Civica."

"Sa ha! 'Tisn't often *that* goes to an Auxiliary. No

offence, 'isn't often it goes to anybody, come to that. Any idea who it was?"

"One of the fire-eating Dacians. I've an idea it was the pennant-bearer." Hirpinius turned quickly to the stranger in their midst. "Fools that we are! Of course you're the one who'd be knowing. . . ." He checked, his eyes suddenly widening at what he saw in Aracos's face, his mouth ajar.

But it was one of the Auxiliaries who said in a tone of awed discovery. "It was you, wasn't it?"

The Corona Civica, the highest award for personal bravery under the Eagles! They were all staring at him now. "You?" someone said incredulously. "You!"

Something flickered far behind the horse breeder's eyes. For a moment he hesitated, then shrugged. "You could say I earned it—yes." There was a note of bitter amusement in his tone, as though he laughed inwardly at an ugly jest against himself.

"But man! Why keep it under your helmet! It isn't exactly a thing to be ashamed of!

"I've no especial reason to talk about it."

"No reason— Oh, come on, lad, don't pretend you're not human."

"See now," Aracos said, "I'm out from under the Eagles' Wings, and all that is in the past. A circle of gilt oak leaves doesn't carry any weight in the hill horse-runs. Let's drop it."

But Gavrus, who seemed the leader among the rest, was already shouting for more wine to celebrate, and one of the Auxiliaries, who had been gazing worshipfully at the unsuspected hero in their midst, leaned forward and said, "Sir—will you tell us about it?"

Aracos's face was flushed, and his pale eyes had reckless sparks in them, but at the eager words he set down his empty wine cup, which the moment before he had been holding up to be refilled with the rest, laughed, and shook his head, and lounged a little unsteadily to his feet. "Maybe another time—another year. Not tonight; I've an early start for the hills in the morning."

Making his somewhat zigzag way back to the leather merchant's house on the outskirts of the town where

he always lodged when he brought the horses down, Aracos cursed inwardly by all the gods he knew.

What a fool he had been to get caught up in the thing at all. He must have been drunker than he realized. But in his inmost places he knew that drunk or sober would have made little difference. He couldn't have sat there and let the boys take up the challenge alone and land themselves in the trouble they were heading for. Yes, but he might at least have had enough wits about him, when the Corona Civica came up, not to let the old story show all over his face. Ah well, it would be half a year before his next trip down from the hills; he'd

probably never see tonight's bunch again, and old Sylvanus who kept the wine shop would forget.

But old Sylvanus did not forget. It made too good a story to tell to customers. Finally Aracos simply shrugged and accepted the situation. Being a hero was always good for a free drink, anyway.

He went on accepting it for two and a half years, and then one autumn day he went down to Isca Silurium with the usual string of remounts, struck his bargain with the garrison horse-master, and took himself to the *Rose and Wine Skin* to wash the dust of the horse-yards out of his throat.

Most of the men crowded about the braziers were strangers to him, but two or three Legionaries whom he knew were grouped together in the far corner. He headed across to join them, but mid-way, a voice exploded in his ear. "Aracos! Now by Jupiter's Thunderbolt, if it isn't Aracos!" And as he looked around, somebody surged into his path; he saw a lean and beaky face with small bright eyes and a coarse, good-humoured mouth, and remembered it from a long time ago.

He felt as though someone had jolted him in the pit of the stomach. "Nasik! What do you do here?" The words sounded stupid in his own ears.

"What should I be doing? The Third Wing's just posted here—back from Pannonia. What do you do?"

"Work for a Horse-Chieftain in the hills. Want any remounts?"

A couple of the older Cavalrymen joined in, grinning and exclaiming at the smallness of the Empire; the younger ones were new since his time. He had a choking desire to turn and thrust his way out into the street again, but that would not stop the thing happening, only mean it happening behind his back. . . .

And then old Sylvanus joined his voice to the rest. "Here's a fine reunion. You'll have been together in that northern fighting, ten years ago? Well now, you're just the lads we want, for we've never yet got him to tell us how he came by the Corona Civica."

A couple of the Legionaries whom Aracos knew, had joined the group and added their voices to the rest. "Now *you* can tell us. Come on now, tell the tale; don't be bashful, my wood anemone!"

Nasik looked from them to Aracos, puzzled; then burst into a shout of laughter. "Corona Civica? It's a jest, isn't it?"

There was a sudden uneasiness among the onlookers, a sharp, startled pause. "A jest? No, why should it be?" someone said.

Nasik broke off his laughter. "You *don't* mean to say —did he tell you he got the Civica?"

Aracos stood quite still, fronting the perplexed and startled faces. There was a little smile on his mouth, as set as though it were carved in stone.

One of the Legionaries, as though defending himself in advance from the charge of being easily duped, said, "One of the Dacians *did* get the Civica in that fight."

"Yes, but not this one. Why, by our Lady of the Foals! He's never been a soldier! He was a medical orderly—an Army butcher's fetch-and-carry man!"

A second Dacian had come up beside the first. "So you thought you'd snap up Felix's cast-off glory, did you? He being dead and not needing it any more!"

42

The wine-shop owner turned a troubled eye on the silent man in their midst. "Well? You'd best be saying something, hadn't you?"

The whole shop was silent to hear his answer, and Aracos, looking round at them with the lazy smile still engraved on his lips, saw that they were not exactly hostile—yet—but the startled perplexity was hardening into disgust, and a hint of the delight of boys watching a cat with a pannikin tied to its tail.

"Surely. It's all perfectly true," he said on a note of amusement.

"But why?"—the wine-shop keeper began.

Aracos shrugged. "It's dull, up in the hills. I wanted

to see if you would be fools enough to believe me—and behold, you were."

A growl of anger answered him, and a small red-haired Legionary got menacingly to his feet. "Why you—you—I'll teach you to make fools of us again!"

But his neighbour seized him by the shoulder and slammed him back on to the bench. "Leave him be. He's not worth getting rounded up by the Watch Patrol for, he looks a much worse fool than we do, anyway."

Aracos turned to the landlord. "I came in for a drink, but I don't much care for the smell in here tonight." He turned, and pushed out into the windy dark, careful not to betray by the set of his shoulders that he heard the shout of laughter and the insults that followed him.

One man among the Dacians had looked up with a start when Nasik first shouted the newcomer's name, and had remained quite still, watching him, through the whole ugly scene that came after. In the somewhat shamefaced silence that followed the laughter, before the shout went up for more wine, he got up with some excuse to his companions, and left the wine shop.

Outside in the street he checked a moment, then turned uphill towards the Dexter Gate of the fortress, still dimly visible in the gusty autumn twilight.

Aracos went downhill towards his lodging. He would not think until he got back to the little room under the roof where he could be alone. He must get away from people, from faces in the light of open doorways.

He came to the leather merchant's door and went in. The daughter of the house came out from an inner room when she heard him; he had always liked her, but tonight he only wanted to be left alone. "You are early," she said, "but supper will be ready soon."

He shook his head. "I am not hungry, Cordaella."

He went past her, up the ladder to the room under the roof. He kicked the door shut behind him, and sat down on the narrow cot. The small earthenware lamp had been lit ready for him, early though he was, and he sat staring at it, not seeing it at all, seeing only the faces in the *Rose and Wine Skin*, hearing the laughter. He wouldn't come down to Isca Silurium again. Old Lyr could make some other arrangement about getting his horses sold. The small sharp pain that came on him sometimes after an especially hard struggle with an unbroken colt, was flickering under his ribs and down his left arm, but he was no more aware of it than he was of the lamp flame.

A long while later, feet came up the ladder, and a hand was on the latch. Cordaella's voice said, "Aracos."

"Go away, Cordaella. I'm not hungry."

"There is someone here to speak with you."

"Tell whoever it is," Aracos said carefully and distinctly, "go to Gehenna!"

There was a murmur of voices. The latch rattled down, the door opened and closed again. "I am sorry," said a quiet voice. "Don't blame the woman; she tried to stop me."

Aracos swung round to see a slight, youngish man with the badge of the Dacian Horse on his belt bucklet, and on the breast of his tunic the entwined serpents of Esculapius that marked him for one of the Medical Corps. Aracos had not consciously noticed him in the wine shop, but he knew him again.

"Get out!"

"Presently."

"Now! Didn't you have enough fun in the *Rose and Wine Skin* that you must come after me for more?"

"I would have been here sooner." The young Medic ignored that. "But had to go back to my quarters to fetch this that I have for you—from Felix."

"Felix is dead," Aracos said dully. "I didn't know, until they said so this evening."

"He died between my hands, two years ago in Pannonia. He bade me take this, and get it to a certain Aracos from Thrace, who was a medical orderly with the Dacians during the Pictish troubles. But you had left the Eagles, and I could not pick up your trail, so I have kept it with my own gear ever since, just on the chance. . . ." He bent and laid on the cot a flat bundle wrapped in a piece of old uniform cloth. "The Empire is a small place, as our friends said."

Aracos took up the bundle and slowly folded back the tattered cloth. Inside was a battered circlet of gilded bronze fashioned into the form of oak leaves. The Corona Civica!

"He said it was yours by rights."

Aracos was silent a few moments, holding the thing gently between his hands. "How did he die?"

"Of wounds taken in driving off an attack on the supply train he was escorting. It was three days later, before he got them into camp. The Gods know how he kept going so long."

In silence the wind gusted against the house, and sent a rustling charge of dry leaves along the court outside.

"I had a feeling," the young Medic said at last, "that you could have said something in your own defence, tonight, and that you deliberately chose to hold it back."

"Did you?" Aracos said, without interest.

He was remembering how it had all begun, the day when he had gone down from his village in the Rhodope Mountains with two other lads, to the recruiting station at Abdera. He could sit a horse with anyone, and it had not occurred to him that the small sharp pain that sometimes caught him in the chest after running uphill was anything to keep him out of the Thracian Cavalry. At Abdera a man with entwined serpents on the breast of his tunic had made each of them in turn run to the sacred olive tree half a mile away and back without stopping, and then laid his ear against their chests and listened to something inside. The other two had been accepted, but not Aracos, though he had run faster than either of them. He wondered later if the man had heard the small pain in his chest that the running had given him.

He hadn't gone home, he would have been shamed, but he found that there was room for other men than warriors under the Eagles, jobs for which you did not have to have anyone listening to your chest. He had liked the man with the entwined serpents, and he was interested by this running and listening; he wanted to know what you could hear inside people that told you they had a pain. And so he had become a medical orderly, with the Thracians at first, then with the Dacian Horse in the far-off province of Britain.

He remembered the great outpost fort of Trimontum on the skirts of its three-peaked hill. He remembered Felix at Cavalry maneuvres, Felix in his pennant-bearer's wolfskin, riding full tilt at the head of the flying squadron, with the long sleeve-pennant of scarlet silk filling with the wind and streaming from its silver serpent-head on the lance point. It was just at the end of those maneuvres that the youngster had been thrown and broken his collar bone; but for that they would probably never have even spoken to each other, for clerks and orderlies and such, Aracos had very soon discovered, were in the Legions and Auxiliaries, but not *of* them. The odd thing was that they were very much alike save that Felix was not so dark, so that for all the seven or eight years difference between them, old Diomedes the camp surgeon called them Castor and Pollux, when Felix came to have his shoulder tended.

He remembered news of unrest filtering down from the north at the end of a long dry summer, the smoke signals feathering the sky; the Dacian Wings under those slim scarlet serpent-pennants riding out to join the 6th

Legion on its forced march northward. He remembered following with the baggage carts in the dust of the marching columns, the heather swimming in the heat, the Pictish harrying that began on the second day; a wolfpack-worrying along their flanks, nightly attacks, scouting patrols that came back bloody and at half strength—one that never came back at all.

He remembered the last night, the knowledge on them all that full battle was coming with the morning; the ordered stir of the camp that never died down all through the tense hours of darkness.

In the first ghost-grey light before a misty dawn, Aracos went down to the latrine trenches beyond the horse lines (the Legions never camped a night without digging such trenches and setting up a stockade) and found Felix there, his wolfskin flung behind him, being violently sick.

"Felix! What is it?"

And then as the boy crouched back on his heels and turned a sweat-streaked face to him, he knew. Felix's squadron had run into trouble more than once during the forced march north, and lost several men; the last time, he had got back with a friend's body with part of the face carried away by a throw-spear, that had still been alive when they set out on the struggle back to camp. That had been once too often.

"Aracos!" The boy was shaking from head to foot, and his teeth chattered as though he had fever. "Aracos! Thank the Gods it's you! Help me—"

Aracos caught his shoulders to steady him. "You're the only one who can do that."

"*You* can—you *can*," Felix gasped.

"How?"

"There must be something. The German Berserks chew leaves of some sort, don't they?" He was beyond

shame; that would come later. "I'd get drunk, but it only makes me sleepy." He bent his face into his hands.

"Stop it!" Aracos said. "You can! I've known men as sick as a cat in the dawn and fight like tigers an hour later."

But when the other looked up again, he knew that he was wrong; he had served with the Eagles long enough to know the look on the face of a man who had reached the end of what he could take. Now, what in the name of Night's Daughters was to be done? Whatever it was, it must be done quickly.

Scarcely realizing what he did, he caught up the wolf-skin and dragged the boy to his feet, and an instant later was crouching with him behind the long mound of earth turned up by the trench diggers. "Listen—I can't give you anything; I can't and I won't!" Then as Felix made a convulsive movement, "No, *listen;* there's only one way out—we're about the same size, and like enough to pass in the dust of fighting. Strip off those leathers."

"You mean you—"

"Yes." Aracos was already yanking at a shoulder buckle.

"You can't."

"I've got to, haven't I? Quick now, off with your breeks." Felix obeyed him, but his eyes had a strange blankness, as though he did not hear. Aracos snatched the breeks from him and dragged them on. "Where's your horse?"

Felix's gaze turned on him with the same blankness.

"Your horse! Where's he picketed?"

"The end of the second line."

"Right." He had the tunic on now, belt, sword belt, the great wolfskin with the head pulled well forward on his brows. "I'm away now. Don't follow for a hundred heart-beats. Then make for the baggage park, lie up in one of the tilt carts nearest to the stockade until I come back, and pray to the Gods, for your own sake as well as mine, that I *do* come back. I'll whistle 'The Girl I Kissed at Clusium.' Don't move until you hear the tune."

The young pennant-bearer still seemed in a daze, but he couldn't wait to make sure he understood. All he could do was to take the youngster's place and hope for a miracle to bring them both through the day without disaster.

Looking back, he still did not know whether he had done right, he only knew that at the time there had seemed nothing else that he could do, and that the miracle had happened. In the ordered bustle of the camp, with the watch fires turning sickly and scarcely a finger of light in the sky, he had got through the issue of food, collected the serpent-pennant from its place with the Cohort Colours and the Eagle itself before the Legate's tent. He had seen it done so often that he made no obvious mistake in the ceremonial; and at half-light, with morning mist thickening among the hills, found himself riding, still unrecognized, behind the Captain at the head of the two wings of Dacian Horse.

The maneuvring for position, the coming and going of Scouts, the hurried Councils of War in the Legate's tent, belonged to yesterday, and he had known nothing of them anyway; his business in life was the medical supplies, not the tactics of hill warfare. And now, as they rode down into the steep river valley across the narrows of which the Tungrians had been standing to all night, and took up their position in reserve behind the steadily forming battle line, his business was with the light sleeve of scarlet silk lifting and stirring from the lance shaft in his hand; to carry out the pennant-bearer's duties with no betraying mistake, and to keep his face hidden.

The rising mist was warm and milky, no freshness in it. The waiting seemed interminable.

And then far ahead, a flurry of shouting broke the silence, and all along the battle line and the ranks of the Reserves ran a tiny ripple of the nerve ends, like an unheard touch on the taut strings of a harp. Somewhere out in front the Roman outposts were already engaged. The shouting came nearer; Pictish war horns were snarling in the mist and the Roman trumpets crowed in answer. And now, to the shouting, was added a clanging and clashing and an earth-shaking rumble that Aracos had heard before, but never from the fighting-ranks, and out of the mist swept a column of war chariots, driven and manned by naked, blue-painted warriors.

They swept across the Roman front, raining down throw-spears which the Legionaries caught for the most part on their shields, and wheeling about on the steepening skirts of the hillside, would have cut in between the first rank and the second. But the Cretan archers posted between the Asturian squadrons on the left flank, wheeled half left as they passed, and loosed a flight of short arrows into their midst, aiming for the teams rather than the men. Team after team came down in kicking chaos and a rending crash of broken yoke-poles and torn-off wheels; the charge lost shape and impetus, and swung away, straightening itself back into some kind of order as it went; and from farther to the right, another column came screaming down upon the Roman battle line. The mist was growing ragged before the light

breeze that had begun to wake with the dawn, and a brief gleam of light from the rising sun slid into the eyes of the archers on the right wing, making their aim less sure; a team went down here and there, but the wild head of the column was into the Tungrian Cavalry before they could be stopped, and in the same instant, from dead ahead, a wave of foot-warriors came yelling out of the mist and flung themselves upon the pilums of the main battle line. The pilums drank blood, but there seemed always more, where the first wave had come from.

Aracos, in his place in the Reserve, the slim scarlet banner hanging limp from the lance-shaft in his hand, was never clear about what happened then. All that his mind kept of the battle, afterwards, was a memory of roaring chaos, until suddenly, unbelievably, the trumpets were sounding for Advance and Follow-Up, and he realized with a leap of the heart, that the Picts were falling back.

The whole struggle was moving northwestward up the curve of the valley. Close beside him, the Dacian Captain snapped an order, and the Cavalry trumpets were yelping. Felix's horse as though catching the surge of excitement, flung up his head with a shrill squeal, and buckled forward under his new rider. But it was not yet fighting time for the Reserves. They only moved forward, keeping station behind the reeling battle line, over dead and wounded men.

The northward surge of the battle slowed and checked once, as though the Picts were making a desperate stand, then rolled on again. The valley swung farther west, rising underfoot, the mist was growing more and more ragged, and suddenly it rolled away like a curtain, still clinging to the northern side of the valley but leaving clear the sheer heather slopes to the south, where a great spur of rock and scree jutted out almost to overhang the narrowing glen.

The man beside him shouted, "Mithras! Look up there!" and following his wildly pointing finger, Aracos saw the crest of the spur swarming with Painted Men.

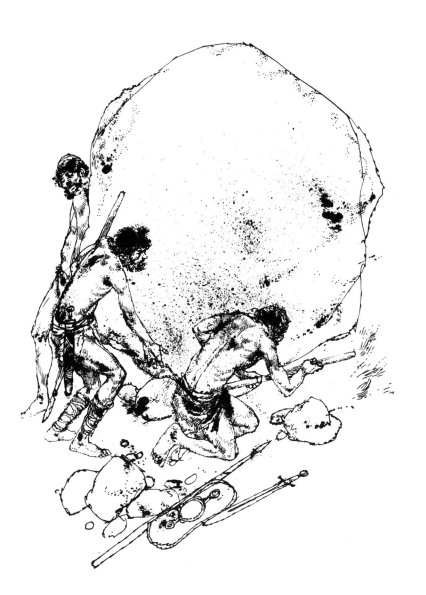

They were prising loose stones out of the heather, and at that very instant the first of these, flung by a naked giant, came whizzing down with the power of a ballista bolt, and somewhere among the surging mass of legionaries a man screamed—half a scream. But a far worse menace was the great boulder, already perilously poised, that topped the crag, round which the Painted Men were labouring with deadly purpose. There were lesser stones to be hauled from about its base, and spear butts made flimsy levers for shifting such a huge mass, but Aracos saw with a sickening lurch of the heart that it was only a matter of time before that vast boulder came crashing down into the midst of the Roman battle-mass, bringing with it, by the look of things, half the hillside as it came.

The Eagles had been led into a trap!

Ahead, the Legionary trumpets were sounding, fiercely urgent. They were echoed by the light notes of the Cavalry trumpets, and three squadrons of Asturians broke away and headed at a slant up the steep hillside, while below them the Centurions fought to get the Cohorts back from the deadly menace of the rock-crowned spur and the great stones already crashing down, and the Pictish warrior-swarm fought as desperately to pen them in.

Suddenly, out of the low sunlight leapt flame that danced up just below the hill shoulder, and spread from point to point into a single curved line of fire, red in the daylight, rippling and undulating towards the horsemen.

"Gods! They've fired the heather!"

In the face of the fire across their path, the Asturians' horses balked and wheeled about, snorting in terror, and flung back from the flames, those in front spreading instant confusion among those behind, and the whole lot, for all the efforts of their riders to check and turn them, stampeding away downhill like unbroken colts. And now the horses on the battle-wings were catching the smell of the fire and the terror of their own kind, flinging this way and that. A few moments more and they would be utterly unmanageable.

"Right! It's us now!" The Dacian Captain gave quick orders to his message-rider: "Get back to the Decurian Sextus and bid him take Second Wing and the hind four squadrons of First forward to hold the battle flank. The rest of First Wing— *With Me!*"

Trumpets yelped again. Aracos drove his heel into the bay's flank and was away at the Captain's side; the wind of their going took the thin scarlet silk and the body of the serpent-pennant filled and rippled out, as he set his horse at the slope, the rest drumming at their heels. Smoke wafted into his eyes, sparks and wisps of burning heather were breaking free and drifting ahead of the main blaze, little red tongues licking up wherever they landed; the thin wall of fire, leaping high now in the morning breeze, rippled like the thin red serpent silk, bending over as though to greet and engulf them. Aracos felt the bay brace and gather himself under him, then hold straight on, no swerving from the flames ahead.

Let the Tungrians laugh in future at the Dacians' tricks!

At the last instant the Captain gave a great shout, then with his cloak flung across nose and mouth, plunged straight into the wall of flame. Aracos galloped at his side, face driven down into the wolfskin. Hideous, blasting heat lapped him round, not a wall of flame but a whole world of flame. He choked into the wolfskin as pain tore at his eyes and throat and lungs—then they were through. There was a stink of singeing horsehide, sparks hung in the rough wolfskin and in the horse's mane, a fringe of flame lengthened the tail of the scarlet serpent. Ahead, the blackened and smoking hillside rose to the spur where the Painted Men still laboured savagely about the great tottering boulder. But away to the right, something moved under cover of the smoke, and next instant a flurry of javelins and sling-stones took the Dacians on the flank. Men and horses went down, Still riding hard for the spur, Aracos was aware of the Captain swaying beside him, clutching at the shaft of a javelin that stuck out from under his collar-bone—choking to him a last order to take them on and clear the spur, before he pitched down among the horses' hooves.

So he took them on, through a vicious squall of sling-stones. Where the ground grew too steep to ride they dropped from the horses and ran on, crouching with heads down behind their light bronze-rimmed bucklers. By the time they reached the spur, hearts and lungs bursting within them, he had no idea how many or how few were still behind him; he had no chance to look

round. He did not even know how many of the horses,
lightened of their riders' weight, had come scrambling
after them, bringing their own weapons, the stallions'
weapons of teeth and trampling hooves, into the fight.
He only knew that the time came when there were no
more Painted Men left alive on the spur, and that the
terrible boulder, swaying as it seemed to every breath,
was still there.

They jammed loose stones under it, and added a few
war-painted bodies for good measure, but to Aracos it

was all hazy, and the only thing that seemed quite real
was the pain in his chest that spread all down his shield-
arm and made a buzzing darkness before his eyes. He
fought the darkness off. If he collapsed now they would
pull off the wolfskin to find where he was wounded,
and see his face. But he never afterwards had the least
idea how they got back to the main force, nor how the
rest of that day went, save that somehow, incredibly, it
ended in a Roman victory, dragged out of what had
nearly been the most hideous defeat.

When things began to seem real again, he was back
in camp, and tending Felix's bay, who had a spear gash

in his flank and looked, like his neighbours in the picket lines, to have been ridden hard all day. There was a vague half-memory in him of having been hunting—not deer or wild ox, but painted men among the heather; and a rather clearer one of setting a wisp of scorched scarlet silk on a lance shaft back in the row of Colours before the Legate's tent.

In the dusk and the ordered confusion, it was not hard to slip away unnoticed, but it could not be long before

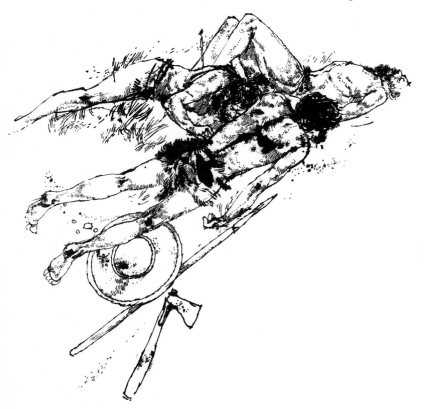

the cry went up for the pennant-bearer of the Dacian Horse. With the wolfskin stripped off and rolled into an unbetraying bundle under one arm, he made for the baggage park, and slipped in among the carts nearest to the stockade. The pain in his chest came and went, like a beast flexing its muscles to spring. He leaned against a wheel, and whistled softly, as well as he could for lack of breath, the first bars of "The Girl I Kissed at Clusium."

There was no answering whistle, but as he listened, something stirred in the next cart. He went to it quickly, and pulling himself up, peered under the tilt.

"Felix!"

Among the sacks and bales, something stirred again, and the pale blur of a face swam in the gloom. "All's over," he whispered, "and all's well. Out now—they'll be missing you at any moment."

"Aracos! Oh, thank the Gods you're back! I was—so afraid you would go down."

"For your sake, or mine?" Aracos said grimly, and then, "Na, forget I said it. Get these on and out with you and take over your empty place. They've killed the Captain. Remember you led First Wing up to clear the Painted People from a hill spur where they were heaving rocks down on the Legion. They fired the heather, but you got through. There's a singed place on the flank of the wolfskin, you'd best rub your face in it."

He was dragging off the leather breeks as he spoke, and tossed them into the cart after tunic and wolfskin.

He heard an inarticulate sound that was almost a sob. The boy had lain there all day long, alone with himself, and the Mother of Foals alone knew what kind of shape he was in now, to carry the thing through; but he could not wait to see. The beast in his chest was getting ready to spring, and he must get clear of the baggage park while he could.

There was a high sweet ringing in his ears, and black webs spun between his eyes and the camp fires, as he turned away towards the wattle shelters beyond a knot of hawthorn scrub where the Medics would be busy with the wounded. He must have been missed, of course; he must think of some reason to give, some story to tell that would not turn anyone's thoughts towards the Dacians' pennant-bearer. . . . He was quite close to one of the fires when the beast in his chest leapt. He took one more step, choking for air against the rending teeth and claws, and had just sense and time left to turn towards the fire as he stumbled to his knees. The black webs spun into solid darkness as he sank forward on to his face among the hot ash. His last thought was that at least the marks of fire on him would be accounted for.

When the darkness ebbed again, he was lying on his back with men standing round him, and one kneeling over him with an ear pressed to his chest, just as the man had done who turned him down for the Thracian Horse.

"He just loomed up out of the darkness and went head first into the fire," someone said. "Has he been at the barley spirit?"

"No," said the man with an ear to his chest, and the voice was that of Diomedes, the surgeon. Then, straightening up, "Poor brute, he must have felt it coming on him and hidden away like a sick animal."

Another voice pointed out, "You heard what these men said; he hasn't just been lying around here all day, sir."

"I said hidden away, not lying around. I imagine he thought the worst was over, and was on his way back to duty when it took him again."

In the end, they had decided that he had some sort of rift in his heart that the strain of the campaign had worsened, and he was invalided out with a small sickness gratuity, just about the time the news came through that Felix had won the Corona Civica for clearing the Picts from the hill spur after the Wing Captain was killed, and thereby most likely saving the Legion.

They had been back at Trimontum leaving the north quiet behind them, a good while by then, and Aracos was going south next day with a returning supply train; south, and out from the service of the Eagles.

Felix had hunted him out, where he had gone down the river glen to make a last small sacrifice at the Altar to Fortune which one of the garrison had put up long ago. The boy looked old and haggard, as though he were the one who had been ill. "I cannot go through with this!" he said desperately.

"Yes, you can."

"I *can't!* I'm going to tell them. I don't care what they do to me, anything would be better than this!"

And Aracos had caught him by the shoulders as he had done once before. "Now listen! The Gods know why I was fool enough to do what I did for you, but this I know; you're not going to undo it all now!"

There had been a long silence, broken only by the voice of the little stream that flowed out from under the shrine, and then Felix had moaned softly, like something with a physical hurt. "I could hack myself to pieces! I don't know what happened and I don't know it won't happen again. . . . If only I could be the one to pay. . . ."

Aracos had tightened his grip. "You'll pay your share, all right. All your life you're going to have to wear that circlet of gilded oak leaves through your shoulder strap, and feel men's eyes on it, and know the truth behind it. Oh, you'll pay, Felix, so we can cry quits."

And he had seen the slack despairing lines of the boy's face tauten, and his head go up, as he took the strain.

"But what will you do?" he asked after a while.

"Stay on in Britain. I spent my first year in the province on garrison duty at Burrium. There's good horse country among the Welsh hills. I might try to get work there. I've my gratuity; I shan't starve while I'm looking for it."

A whirling moth blundered into the lamp flame, and fell away, singed and sodden, and Aracos was in the present again. He was alone, though he had not heard the young Medic go, and still holding between his hands the battered circlet of gilded oak leaves. In one place the bronze showed through, where the gilt was all rubbed away by the shoulder strap through which it had been worn for more than eight years.

Again he remembered Felix's set face. Oh yes, Felix
had paid his price. And in the end—what had the Medic
said? "He died between my hands, two years ago in
Pannonia . . . of wounds taken in driving off an attack
on the supply train he was escorting. It was three days
later, before he got them into camp. The Gods know
how he kept going so long."

A small inward bitterness that had been with Aracos

for ten years suddenly fell away. He had been worth saving, that boy. He thought with a detached interest, as though it concerned somebody else and not himself at all, that now he could tell the truth, and be believed. But the thought remained detached. One didn't betray a friend merely because he was dead.

But he knew, for no very clear reason, that because that wild day's work ten years ago had not been wasted, because Felix had died in the way he had done, and dying, had sent him the battered circlet of oak leaves, he would bring down the remounts again next spring, and go to the *Rose and Wine Skin* again—and again— and again, until the story grew too threadbare to be bothered with any more, and he had come out beyond it.

He folded the Corona Civica carefully in its bit of old cloth again, and getting up, opened the door and called down the ladder, "Cordaella! Is there any supper left?"

A Crown of Wild Olive

It was still early in the day, but already it was growing hot; the white dry heat of the Greek summer; and the faint off-shore wind that made it bearable had begun to feather the water, breaking and blurring the reflections of the galleys lying at anchor in Pireaus Harbour.

Half Athens, it seemed, had crowded down to the port to watch the *Paralos*, the State Galley, sail for the Isthmus, taking their finest athletes on the first stage of their journey to Olympia.

Every fourth summer it happened; every fourth

summer for more than three hundred years. Nothing was allowed to stand in the way, earthquake or pestilence or even war—even the long and weary war which, after a while of uneasy peace, had broken out again last year between Athens and Sparta.

Back in the spring the Herald had come, proclaiming the Truce of the Games; safe conduct through all lands

and across all seas, both for the athletes and for those who went to watch them compete. And now, from every Greek state and from colonies and settlements all round the Mediterranean, the athletes would be gathering. . . .

Aboard the *Paralos* was all the ordered bustle of departure, ropes being cast off, rowers in their places at the oars. The Athenian athletes and their trainers with them had gathered on the afterdeck. Amyntas, son of Ariston, had drawn a little apart from the rest. He was the youngest there, still several months from his eighteenth birthday and somewhat conscious that he had not yet sacrificed his boy's long hair to Apollo, while the rest, even of those entered for the boys' events —you counted as a boy at Olympia until you were

twenty—were already short-haired and doing their Military Service. A few of them even had scars gained in border clashes with the Spartans, to prove that their real place, whatever it might be on the race track or in the wrestling pit, was with the men. Amyntas envied them. He was proud that he had been picked so young to run for Athens in the Boys' Double Stade, the Four Hundred Yards. But he was lonely. He was bound in with all the others by their shared training; but they were bound together by something else, by another kind of life, other loyalties and shared experiences and private jokes, from which he was still shut out.

The last ropes holding ship to shore were being cast off now. Fathers and brothers and friends on the jetty were calling last moment advice and good luck wishes. Nobody called to Amyntas, but he turned and looked back to where his father stood among the crowd. Ariston had been a runner too in his day, before a Spartan spear wound had stiffened his left knee and spoiled his own hopes of an Olympic Olive Crown. Everyone said that he and Amyntas were very alike, and looking back now at the slight dark man who still held himself like a runner, Amyntas hoped with a warm rush of pride, that they were right. He wished he had said so, before he came aboard; there were so many things he would have liked to have said, but he was even more tongue-tied with his father than he was with the rest of the world, when it came to saying the things that mattered. Now, as the last ropes fell away, he flung up his hand in salute, and tried to put them all into one wordless message. "I'll run the best race that's in me, Father—and if the Gods let me win it, I'll remember that I'm winning for us both."

Among the waving crowd, his father flung up an answering hand, as though he had somehow received the message. The water was widening between ship and shore; the Bos'n struck up the rowing time on his flute, and the rowers bent to their oars, sending the *Paralos* through the water towards the harbour mouth. Soon the crowd on shore was only a shingle of dark and coloured and white along the waterfront. But far off beyond the roofs of the warehouses and the covered docks, a flake of light showed where high over Athens the sunlight flashed back from the upraised spear-blade of the great Athene of the Citadel, four miles away.

They were out round the mole now, the one sail broke out from the mast, and they headed for the open gulf.

That night they beached the *Paralos* and made camp on the easternmost point of the long island of Salamis; and not long past noon next day they went ashore at the Isthmus and took horse for Corinth on the far side, where a second galley was waiting to take them down the coast. At evening on the fifth day they rode down into the shallow valley where Olympian Zeus the Father of Gods and men had his sanctuary, and where the Sacred Games were celebrated in his honour.

What with the long journey and the strangeness of

everything, Amyntas took in very little of that first evening. They were met and greeted by the Council of the Games, whose president made them a speech of welcome, after which the Chief Herald read them the rules. And afterwards they ate the evening meal in the athletes' mess; food that seemed to have no more taste nor substance than the food one eats in a dream. Then the dream blended away into a dark nothingness of sleep that took Amyntas almost before he had lain down on the narrow stretcher bed in the athletes' lodging, which would be his for the next month.

He woke to the first dappled fingers of sunlight shafting in through the doorway of his cell. They wavered and danced a little, as though broken by the shadows of tree branches. Somewhere further down the valley a cuckoo was calling, and the world was real again, and his, and new as though it had been born that morning. He rolled over, and lay for a few moments, his hands behind his head, looking up at the bare rafters; then shot off the bed and through the doorway in one swallow-dive of movement, to sluice his head and shoulders in the icy water trickling from the mouth of a stone bull into a basin just outside. He came up for air, spluttering and shaking the water out of his eyes. For a moment he saw the colonnaded court and the plane tree arching over the basin through a splintered brightness of flying droplets. And then suddenly, in the brightness, there stood a boy of about his own age, who must have come

out of the lodging close behind him. A boy with a lean
angular body, and a dark, bony face under a shock of
hair like the crest of an ill-groomed pony. For a long
moment they stood looking at each other. Then Amyntas moved aside to let the other come to the conduit.

As the stranger ducked his head and shoulders under

the falling water, Amyntas saw his back. From shoulder to flank it was criss-crossed with scars, past the purple stage but not yet faded to the silvery white that they would be in a few years' time; pinkish scars that looked as though the skin was still drawn uncomfortably tight over them.

He must have made some betraying sound or movement, because the other boy ducked out from under the water, thrusting the wet russet hair back out of his eyes, and demanded curtly, "Have you never seen a Spartan back before?"

So that was it. Amyntas, like everyone else, had heard dark stories of Spartan boys flogged, sometimes to death, in a ritual test of courage, before the shrine of Artemis Orthia, the Lady of the Beasts.

"No," he said, "I am Athenian." And did not add that he hoped to see plenty of Spartan backs when once he had started his military service. It was odd, the cheap jibe came neatly into his head, and yet he did not even want to speak it. It was as though here at Olympia, the Truce of the Games was not just a rule of conduct, but something in one's heart. Instead, he added, "And my name is Amyntas."

They seemed to stand confronting each other for a long time. The Spartan boy had the look of a dog sniffing at a stranger's fist and taking his own time to make sure whether it was friendly. Then he smiled; a slow, rather grave smile, but unexpectedly warm. "And mine is Leon."

"And you're a runner." Amyntas was taking in his build and the way he stood.

"I am entered for the Double Stade."

"Then we race against each other."

Leon said in the same curt tone, "May we both run a good race."

"And meanwhile,—when did you arrive, Leon?"

"Last night, the same as you."

Amyntas, who usually found it nearly as difficult to talk to strangers as he did to his own father, was surprised to hear himself saying, "Then you'll have seen no more of Olympia than I have. Shall we go and get some clothes on and have a look round?"

But by that time more men and boys were coming out into the early sunshine, yawning and stretching the sleep out of their muscles. And Amyntas felt a hand clamp down on his shoulder, and heard the voice of Hippias his trainer, "Oh no you don't, my lad! Five days' break in training is long enough, and I've work for you before you do any sightseeing!"

After that, they were kept hard at it, on the practice track and in the wrestling school that had the names of past Olympic victors carved on the colonnade walls. For the last month's training for the Games had to be done at Olympia itself; and the last month's training was hard, in the old style that did not allow for rest days in the modern fashion that most of the Athenian trainers favoured. Everything at Olympia had to be done the old way, even to clearing the stadium of its four years' growth of grass and weeds and spreading it with fresh sand. At other Crown Games, the work was done by paid labourers, but here, the contending athletes must do it themselves, to the glory of the Gods, as they had done it in the far-off days when the Games were new. Some of them grumbled a good deal and thought it was time that the Priests of Zeus and the Council of the

Games brought their ideas up to date; but to Amyntas there seemed to be a sort of rightness about the thing as it was.

His training time was passed among boys from Corinth and Epidauros, Rhodes and Samos and Macedon. At first they were just figures in outline, like people seen too far off to have faces, whom he watched with interest at track work, at javelin or discus throwing or in the wrestling pit, trying to judge their form as he knew they were trying to judge his and each other's. But gradually as the early days went by, they changed into people with faces, with personal habits, and likes and dislikes, suffering from all the strains and stresses of the last weeks before the Games. But even before those first few days were over, he and the Spartan boy had drifted into a companionable pattern of doing things together. They would sluice each other down, squatting in the stone hip-baths in the washing room after practice, and scrape the mess of rubbing oil and sand off each other's backs—it took Amyntas a little while to learn to scrape the bronze blade of the strigil straight over the scars on Leon's back as though they were not there—and when they took their turn at scraping up the four years' growth of grass and sun-dried herbs from the stadium, they generally worked together, sharing one of the big rush carrying-baskets between them. And in the evenings, after the day's training was over, or in the hot noonday break when most people stretched themselves out in the shade of the

plane trees for sleep or quiet talk, they seemed, more
often than not, to drift into each other's company.

Once or twice they went to have a look at the town
of tents and booths that was beginning to spring up all
round the Sacred Enclosure and the Gymnasium buildings—for a Games Festival drew many people beside
those who came to compete or to watch; merchants and

wine sellers and fortune tellers, poets determined to get poems heard, horse dealers from Corinth and Cyrene, goldsmiths and leather-workers, philosophers gathering for the pleasure of arguing with each other, sword and fire swallowers, and acrobats who could dance on their hands to the soft notes of Phrygian pipes. But Leon did not much like the crowded noisy tent-ground; and most often they wandered down to the river that flung its loop about the south side of Olympia. It had shrunk now

in the summer heat, to little more than a chain of pools in the middle of its pale dried-out pebbly bed; but there was shade under the oleander trees, and generally a whisper of moving air. And lying on the bank in the shade was free. It had dawned on Amyntas quite early that the reason Leon did not like the fairground was that he had no money. The Spartans did not use money, or at least, having decided that it was a bad thing, they had no coinage but iron bars so big and heavy that nobody could carry them about, or even keep a store at home that was worth enough to be any use. They were very proud of their freedom from wealth, but it made life difficult at a gathering such as this, when they had to mix with people from other states. Leon covered up by being extremely scornful of the gay and foolish things for sale in the merchants' booths, and the acrobats who passed the bowl round for contributions after their performance; but he was just that shade too scornful to be convincing. And anyway, Amyntas had none too much money himself, to get him through the month.

So they went to the river. They were down there one hot noontide something over a week after they had first arrived at Olympia; Amyntas lying on his back, his hands behind his head, squinting up into the dark shadow-shapes of the oleander branches against the sky; Leon sitting beside him with his arms round his updrawn knees, staring out into the dazzle of sunlight over the open riverbed. They had been talking runners' talk, and suddenly Amyntas said, "I was watching the Corinthian

making his practice run this morning. I don't *think* we have either of us much to fear from him."

"The Rhodian runs well," said Leon, not bringing back his gaze from the white dance of sunlight beyond the oleanders.

"But he uses himself up too quickly. He's the kind that makes all the front running at first, and has nothing left for the home stretch. Myself, I'd say that red-headed barbarian from Macedon had the better chance."

"He's well enough for speed; and he knows how and when to use it. . . . What do you give for Nikomedes' chances?"

"Nikomedes?—The boy from Megara? It's hard to say. Not much, from the form he's shown so far; but we've only seen him at practice, and he's the sort that sometimes catches fire when it comes to the real thing. . . ."

There was a long silence between them, and they heard the churring of the grasshoppers, like the heat-shimmer turned to sound. And then Amyntas said, "I think you are the one I have most to fear."

And Leon turned his head slowly and looked down at him, and said, "Have you only just woken to that? I knew the same thing of *you*, three days ago."

And they were both silent again, and suddenly a little shocked. You might think that kind of thing, but it was best not to put it into words.

Leon made a quick sign with his fingers to avert ill luck; and Amyntas scrambled to his feet. "Come on, it's time we were getting back." They were both laughing, but a little breathlessly. Leon dived to his feet also, and shot ahead as they went up through the riverside scrub. But next instant, between one flying leap and the next, he stumbled slightly, and checked; then turned back, stooping to search for something among the dusty root-tangle of dry grass and camomile. Amyntas, swerving just in time to avoid him, checked also.

"What is it?"

"Something sharp. . . ." Leon pulled out from where it had lain half-buried, the broken end of a sickle blade that looked as though it might have lain there since the last Games. "Seems it's not only the Stadium that needs clearing up." He began to walk on, carrying the jagged fragment in his hand. But Amyntas saw the blood on the dry ground where he had been standing.

"You have cut your foot."

"I know," Leon said, and went on walking.

"Yes, I *know* you know. Let me look at it."

"It's only a scratch."

"All the same—show me."

Leon stood on one leg, steadying himself with a hand on Amyntas' shoulder, and turned up the sole of his foot. "Look then. You can hardly see it."

There was a cut on the hard brown sole, not long, but deep, with the blood welling slowly. Amyntas said in sudden exasperation, "Haven't you *any* sense? Oh we all know about the Spartan boy with the fox under his cloak, and nobody but you Spartans thinks it's a partic-

ularly clever or praiseworthy story; but if you get dirt into that cut, you'll like enough have to scratch from the race!"

Leon suddenly grinned. "Nobody but we Spartans understand that story. But about the dirt, you could be right."

"I could. And that bit of iron is dirty enough for a start. Best get the wound cleaned up, in the river before we go back to the Gymnasium. Then your trainer can take over."

So with Leon sitting on a boulder at the edge of the shrunken river, Amyntas set to work with ruthless thoroughness to clean the cut. He pulled it open, the cool water running over his hands, and a thin thread of crimson fronded away downstream. It would help clean the wound to let it bleed a little; but after a few moments the bleeding almost stopped. No harm in making sure; he ducked his head to the place, sucked hard and spat crimson into the water. Then he tore a strip from the skirt of his tunic; he would have commandeered Leon's own—after all it was Leon's foot—but he knew that the Spartan boys were only allowed to own one tunic at a time; if he did that, Leon would be left without a respectable tunic to wear at the Sacrifices. He lashed the thin brown foot tightly. "Now—put your arm over my shoulder and try to keep your weight off the cut as much as you can."

"Cluck, cluck, cluck!" said Leon, but he did as Amyntas said.

97

As they skirted the great open space of the Hippodrome, where the chariot races would be held on the second day of the Games, they came up with a couple of the Athenian contingent, strolling under the plane trees. Eudorus the wrestler looked round and his face quickened with concern, "Run into trouble?"

"Ran into the remains of a sickle blade someone left in the long grass," Amyntas said, touching the rusty bit of metal he had taken from Leon and stuck in his own belt. "It's near the tendon, but it's all right, so long as there's no dirt left in it."

"Near the tendon, eh? Then we'd best be taking no chances." Eudorus looked at Leon. "You are Spartan, I think?—Amyntas, go and find the Spartan trainer; I'll take over here." And then to Leon again, "Will you allow me to carry you up to the lodging? It seems the simplest way."

Amyntas caught one parting glimpse of Leon's rigid face as Eudorus lifted him, lightly as a ten-year-old, and set off towards the gymnasium buildings; and laughter caught at his stomach; but mixed with the laughter was sympathy. He knew he would have been just as furious in Leon's place. All this fuss and to-do over a cut that would have been nothing in itself—if the Games had not been only three weeks off.

He set off in search of the trainer.

In the middle of that night, Amyntas woke up with a thought already shaped and complete in his mind. It was an ugly thought, and it sat on his chest and mouthed at him slyly. "Leon is the one you have most to fear. If Leon is out of the race. . . ."

He looked at it in the darkness, feeling a little sick. Then he pushed it away, and rolled over on to his face

with his head in his arms, and after a while he managed to go back to sleep again.

Next day, as soon as he could slip away between training sessions, he went out into the growing town of tents and booths, and found a seller of images and votive offerings, and bought a little bronze bull with silvered horns. It cost nearly all the money that he had to spare, so that he would not now be able to buy the hunting knife with silver inlay on the hilt, that had caught his fancy a day or two since. With the little figure in his hand, he went to the Sacred Enclosure, where, among altars shaded by plane trees, and statues of Gods and Olympic heroes, the great Temple of Zeus faced the older and darker house of Hera his wife.

Before the Temple of Zeus, the ancient wild olive trees from which the victors' crowns were made cast dapple-shade across the lower steps of the vast portico. He spoke to the attendant priest in the deep threshold shadows beyond.

"I ask leave to enter and make an offering."

"Enter then, and make the offering," the man said.

And he went through into the vastness of the Temple itself, where the sunlight sifting through under the acanthus roof tiles made a honeycomb glow that hung high in the upper spaces and flowed down the gigantic columns, but scarcely touched the pavement under foot, so that he seemed to wade in cool shadows. At the far end, sheathed in gold and ivory, his feet half lost in shadows, his head gloried with the dim radiance of the

upper air, stern and serene above the affairs of mortal men, stood the mighty statue of the God himself. Olympian Zeus, in whose honour the Sacred Games had been held for more than three hundred years. Three hundred years, such a little while; looking up at the heart-stilling face above him, Amyntas wondered if the God had even noticed yet, that they were begun. Everything in the God's House was so huge, even time. . . . For a moment his head swam, and he had no means of judging the size of anything, even himself, here where all the known landmarks of the world of men were left behind. Only one thing, when he looked down at it, remained constant in size; the tiny bronze bull with the silvered horns that he held in his hand.

He went forward to the first of the Offering Tables before the feet of the gigantic statue, and set it down. Now, the tables were empty and waiting, but by the end of the festival, they would be piled with offerings; small humble ones like his own, and silver cups and tripods of gilded bronze to be taken away and housed in the Temple treasury. On the eve of the Games they would begin to fill up, with votive offerings made for the most part by the athletes themselves, for their own victory, or the victory of a friend taking part in a different event. Amyntas was not making the offering for his own victory, nor for Leon's. He was not quite sure why he was making it, but it was for something much more complicated than victory in the Double Stade. With one finger still resting on the back of the

little bronze bull, he sent up the best prayer he could sort out from the tangle of thoughts and feelings within himself. "Father of all things, Lord of these Sacred Games, let me keep a clean heart in this, let me run the best race that is in me, and think of nothing more."

Outside again, beyond the dapple-shade of the olive trees, the white sunlight fell dazzling across his eyes, and the world of men, in which things had returned to their normal size, received him back; and he knew that Hippias was going to be loudly angry with him for having missed a training session. But unaccountably, everything, including Hippias' anger, seemed surprisingly small.

Leon had to break training for three days, at least so far as track-work was concerned; and it was several more before he could get back into full training; so for a while it was doubtful whether he would be able to take his place in the race. But with still more than a week to go, both his trainer and the Doctor-Priest of Asklepius declared him fit, and his name remained on the list of entrants for the Double Stade.

And then it was the first day of the Festival; the day of solemn dedication, when each competitor must go before the Council to be looked over and identified, and take the Oath of the Games before the great bronze statue of Zeus of the Thunderbolts.

The day passed. And next morning before it was light, Amyntas woke to hear the unmistakable, unforgettable voice of the crowds gathering in the Stadium. A shapeless surf of sound, pricked by the sharper cries of the jugglers and acrobats, and the sellers of water and honeycakes, myrtle and victors' ribbons calling their wares.

This was the day of the Sacred Procession; the Priests and Officials, the beasts garlanded for sacrifice, the athletes marching into the waiting Stadium, while the Herald proclaimed the name and state of each one as he passed the rostrum. Amyntas, marching in with the Athenians, heard his own name called, and Leon's, among names from Samos and Cyrene, Crete and Corinth and Argos and Megara. And he smelled the incense on the morning air, and felt for the first time, under his swelling pride in being Athenian, the thread of his own Greekness interwoven with the Greekness of all those others. This must have been, a little, the thing their Great Grandfathers had felt when they stood together, shield to shield, to hurl back the whole strength of invading Persia, so that they might remain free. That had been in a Games year, too. . . .

The rest of that day was given over to the chariot and horse races; and that night Amyntas went to his sleeping cell with the thunder of hooves and wheels still sounding somewhere behind his ears. He seemed to hear it in his dreams all night, but when he woke in the morning, it had turned into the sound that he had woken to yesterday, the surf-sound of the gathering crowd. But this morning it had a new note for him, for this was the Day, and the crowd that was gathering out there round the Stadium was his crowd, and his belly tightened and the skin prickled at the back of his neck as he heard it.

He lay for a few moments, listening, then got up and went out to the conduit. Leon came out after him as he had done that first morning of all, and they sluiced down as best they could. The water barely dribbled from the mouth of the stone bull now, for with the vast gathering of people, and the usual end-of-summer drought, the water shortage was getting desperate, as it always did by the time the Festival days arrived.

"How is the foot?" Amyntas asked.

"I can't remember where the cut was, unless I look for it."

They stood looking at each other, the friendship that they had never put into words trying to find some way to reach across from one to the other.

"We cannot even wish each other luck," Amyntas said at last, helplessly.

And Leon said, almost exactly as he had said it at their first meeting, "May both of us run a good race."

They reached out and touched hands quickly and went their separate ways.

The next time they saw each other, they were waiting oiled and naked for the track, with the rest of the Double Stade boys just outside the arched way into the Stadium. The Dolichus, the long distance race, and the Stade had been run, each with its boys' race immediately after. Now the trumpet was sounding to start the Double Stade. Amyntas' eyes went to meet Leon's, and found the Spartan boy's slightly frowning gaze waiting for him. He heard the sudden roar of the crowd, and his belly lifted and tightened. A little stir ran through the waiting boys; the next time the starting trumpet sounded, the next time the crowd gave that roar, it would be for them. Hippias was murmuring last-minute advice into Amyntas' ear, but he did not hear a word of it. . . . He was going out there before all those thousands upon thousands of staring eyes and yelling mouths, and he was going to fail. Not just fail to win the race, but *fail*. His belly was churning now, his heart banging away right up in his throat so that it almost choked him. His mouth was dry and the palms of his hands were wet; and the beginnings of panic were whimpering up in him. He looked again at Leon, and saw him run the tip of his tongue over his lips as though they were suddenly dry. It was the first time he had ever known the Spartan boy to betray anything of what was going on inside him; and the sight gave him a sense of companionship that somehow steadied him. He began to take deep quiet breaths, as he had been taught, and the rising panic quietened and sank away.

The voice of the crowd was rising, rising to a great roar; the Men's Double Stade was over. He heard the Herald crying the name of the winner, and another roar from the crowd; and then the runners were coming out through the arched entrance; and the boys pressed back to let them past, filthy with sweat and sand and oil. Amyntas looked at the face of the man with the victor's ribbons knotted round his head and arms, and saw that it was grey and spent and oddly peaceful.

"Now it's us!" someone said; and the boys were sprinting down the covered way, out into the open sun-drenched space of the Stadium.

The turf banks on either side of the broad track, and the lower slopes of the Kronon Hill that looked down upon it were packed with a vast multitude of onlookers. Half-way down on the right-hand side, raised above the tawny grass on which everybody else sat, were the benches for the Council, looking across to the white marble seat opposite, where the Priestess of Demeter, the only woman allowed at the Games, sat as still as though she herself were carved from marble, among all the jostling, swaying, noisy throng. Men were raking over the silver sand on the track. The trumpeter stood ready.

They had taken their places now behind the long white limestone curbs of the starting line. The Umpire was calling: "Runners! Feet to the lines!"

Amyntas felt the scorching heat of the limestone as he braced the ball of his right foot into the shaped groove. All the panic of a while back had left him, he felt light, and clear headed, and master of himself. He had drawn the sixth place, with Leon on his left and the boy from Megara on his right. Before him the track stretched white in the sunlight, an infinity of emptiness and distance.

The starting trumpet yelped; and the line of runners sprang forward like a wave of hunting dogs slipped from the leash.

Amyntas was running smoothly and without hurry. Let the green front-runners push on ahead. In this heat they would have burned themselves out before they reached the turning post. He and Leon were running neck and neck with the red-headed Macedonian. The Rhodian had gone ahead now after the front-runners, the rest were still bunched. Then the Corinthian made a sprint and passed the boy from Rhodes, but fell back almost at once. The white track was reeling back underfoot, the turning post racing towards them. The bunch had thinned out, the front-runners beginning to drop back already; and as they came up towards the turning post, first the boy from Macedon, and then Nikomedes catching fire at last, slid into the lead, with Amyntas and Leon close behind them. Rounding the post, Amyntas skidded on the loose sand and Leon went ahead; and it was then, seeing the lean scarred back ahead of him, that Amyntas lengthened his stride, knowing that the time had come to run. They were a quarter of the way down the home lap when they passed Nikomedes; the Megaran boy had taken fire too late. They were beginning to overhaul the redhead; and Amyntas knew in his bursting heart that unless something unexpected happened, the race must be between himself and Leon. Spartan and Macedonian were going neck and neck now; the position held for a few paces, and then the redhead gradually fell behind. Amyntas was going all out, there was pain in his breast and belly and in the backs of his legs, and he did not know where his next breath was coming from; but still the thin

scarred back was just ahead. The crowd were beginning to give tongue, seeing the two come through to the front; a solid roar of sound that would go on rising now until they passed the finishing post. And then suddenly Amyntas knew that something was wrong; Leon was labouring a little, beginning to lose the first keen edge of his speed. Snatching a glance downward, he saw a fleck of crimson in the sand. The cut had re-opened.

His body went on running, but for a sort of splinter of time his head seemed quite apart from the rest of him, and filled with an unmanageable swirl of thoughts and feelings. Leon might have passed the top of his speed anyway, it might be nothing to do with his foot— But the cut *had* re-opened. . . . To lose the race because of a cut foot. . . . It would be so easy not to make that final desperate effort that his whole body was crying out against. Then Leon would keep his lead. . . . And at the same time another part of himself was remembering his father standing on the quayside at Piraeus as the *Paralos* drew away—crying out that he was not running only for himself but for Athens, his City and his people. . . . A crown of wild olive would be the greatest thing that anyone could give to his friend. . . . It would be to insult Leon to let him win . . . you could not do that to your friend. . . . And then, like a clean cold sword of light cutting through the swirling tangle of his thoughts, came the knowledge that greater than any of these things were the Gods. These were the Sacred Games, not some mere struggle between boys in the gymnasium. For one fleeting instant of time he remembered himself standing in the Temple before the great statue of Zeus, holding the tiny bronze bull with the silvered horns. "Let me run the best race that is in me, and think of nothing more."

He drove himself forward in one last agonizing burst of speed, he was breathing against knives, and the roar of the blood in his ears drowned the roar of the crowd. He was level with Leon—and then there was nothing ahead of him but the winning post.

The onlookers had crowded right down towards it; even above the howl of the blood in his head he heard them now, roar on solid roar of sound, shouting him in to victory. And then Hippias had caught him as he plunged past the post; and he was bending over the trainer's arm, bending over the pain in his belly, snatching at his breath and trying not to be sick. People were throwing sprigs of myrtle, he felt them flicking and falling on his head and shoulders. The sickness eased a little and his head was clearing; he began to hear friendly voices congratulating him; and Eudorus came shouldering through the crowd with a coloured ribbon to tie round his head. But when he looked round for Leon, the Spartan boy had been swept away by his trainer. And a queer desolation rose in Amyntas and robbed his moment of its glory.

Afterwards in the changing room, some of the other boys came up to congratulate him. Leon did not come;

but when they had cleaned off the sand and oil and sweat, and sluiced down with the little water that was allowed them, Amyntas hung about, sitting on the well kerb outside while the trainer finished seeing to his friend's foot. And when Leon came out at last, he came straight across to the well, as though they had arranged to meet there. His face was as unreadable as usual.

"You will have cooled off enough by now, do you want to drink?" Amyntas said, mainly because somebody had to say something; and dipped the bronze cup that always stood on the well kerb in the pail that he had drawn.

Leon took the cup from him and drank, and sat down on the well kerb beside him. As Amyntas dipped the cup again and bent his head to drink in his turn, the ends of the victor's ribbon fell forward against his cheek, and he pulled it off impatiently, and dropped it beside the well.

"Why did you do that?" Leon said.

"I shall never be sure whether I won that race."

"The judges are not often mistaken, and I never heard yet of folk tying victors' ribbons on the wrong man."

Amyntas flicked a thumb at Leon's bandaged foot. "You know well enough what I mean. I'll never be sure whether I'd have come first past the post, if that hadn't opened up again."

Leon looked at him a moment in silence, then flung up his head and laughed. "Do you really think that could make any difference? It would take more than a cut foot to slow me up, Athenian!—You ran the better race, that's all."

It was said on such a harsh, bragging note that in the first moment Amyntas felt as though he had been struck in the face. Then he wondered if it was the overwhelming Spartan pride giving tongue, or simply Leon, hurt and angry and speaking the truth. Either way, he was too tired to be angry back again. And which ever it was, it seemed that Leon had shaken it off already. The noon break was over, and the trumpets were sounding for the Pentathlon.

"Up!" Leon said, when Amyntas did not move at once. "Are you going to let it be said that your own event is the only one that interests you?"

They went, quickly and together, while the trainer's eye was off them, for Leon was under orders to keep off his foot. And the people cheered them both when they appeared in the Stadium. They seldom cared much for a good loser, but Leon had come in a close second, and they had seen the blood in the sand.

The next day the heavyweight events were held; and then it was the last day of all, the Crowning Day. Ever after, Amyntas remembered that day as a quietness after great stress and turmoil. It was not, in truth, much less noisy than the days that had gone before. The roaring of the Stadium crowds was gone; but in the town of tents the crowds milled to and fro. The jugglers with knives and the eaters of fire shouted for an audience and the merchants cried their wares; and within the Sacred

Enclosure where the winners received their crowns and made their sacrifices before the Temples of Zeus and Hera, there were the flutes and the songs in praise of the victors, and the deep-voiced invocations to the Gods.

But in Amyntas himself, there was the quiet. He remembered the Herald crying his name, and the light springy coolness of the wild olive crown as it was pressed down on his head; and later, the spitting light of pine torches under the plane trees, where the officials and athletes were feasting. And he remembered most, looking up out of the torchlight, and seeing, high and remote above it all, the winged tripods on the roof of the great Temple, outlined against the light of a moon two days past the full.

The boys left before the feasting was over; and in his sleeping cell Amyntas heard the poets singing in praise of some chariot team, and the applause, while he gathered his few belongings together, ready for tomorrow's early start, and stowed his olive crown among them. Already the leaves were beginning to wilt after the heat of the day. The room that had seemed so strange the first night, was familiar now; part of himself; and after tonight it would not know him anymore.

Next morning in all the hustle of departure, he and Leon contrived to meet and slip off for a little on their own.

The whole valley of Olympia was a chaos of tents and booths being taken down, merchants as well as athletes and onlookers making ready for the road. But the Sacred

Enclosure itself was quiet, and the gates stood open. They went through, into the shade of the olive trees before the Temple of Zeus. A priest making the morning offering at a side altar looked at them; but they seemed to be doing no harm, and to want nothing, so he let them alone. There was a smell of frankincense in

the air, and the early morning smell of last night's heavy dew on parched ground. They stood among the twisted trunks and low-hanging branches, and looked at each other and did not know what to say. Already they were remembering that there was war between Athens and Sparta, that the Truce of the Games would last them back to their own states, but no further; and the longer the silence lasted, the more they remembered.

From beyond the quiet of the Enclosure came all the sounds of the great concourse breaking up; voices calling, the stamping of impatient horses. "By this time tomorrow everyone will be gone," Amyntas said at last. "It will be just as it was before we came, for another four years."

"The Corinthians are off already."

"Catching the cool of the morning for those fine chariot horses," Amyntas said, and thought, There's so little time, why do we have to waste it like this?

"One of the charioteers had that hunting knife with the silver inlay. The one you took a fancy to. Why didn't you buy it after all?"

"I spent the money on something else." For a moment Amyntas was afraid that Leon would ask what. But the other boy only nodded and let it go.

He wished suddenly that he could give Leon something, but there was nothing among his few belongings that would make sense in the Spartan's world. It was a world so far off from his own. Too far to reach out, too far to call. Already they seemed to be drifting away from each other, drifting back to a month ago, before they had even met. He put out a hand quickly, as though to hold the other boy back for one more moment, and Leon's hand came to meet it.

"It has been good. All this month it has been good," Leon said.

"It has been good," Amyntas agreed. He wanted to say, "Until the next Games, then." But manhood and military service were only a few months away for both of them; if they did meet at another Games, there would be the faces of dead comrades, Spartan or Athenian, between them; and like enough, for one of them or both, there might be no other Games. Far more likely, if they ever saw each other again, it would be over the tops of their shields.

He had noticed before how, despite their different worlds, he and Leon sometimes thought the same thing at the same time, and answered each other as though the thought had been spoken. Leon said in his abrupt, dead-level voice, "The Gods be with you, Amyntas, and grant that we never meet again."

They put their arms round each other's necks and strained fiercely close for a moment, hard cheekbone against hard cheekbone.

"The Gods be with you, Leon."

And then Eudorus was calling, "Amyntas! Amyntas! We're all waiting!"

And Amyntas turned and ran—out through the gateway of the Sacred Enclosure, towards where the Athenian party were ready to start, and Eudorus was already coming back to look for him.

As they rode up from the Valley of Olympia and took the tracks towards the coast, Amyntas did not look back. The horses' legs brushed the dry dust-grey scrub beside the track, and loosed the hot aromatic scents of wild lavender and camomile and lentisk upon the air. A yellow butterfly hovered past, and watching it out of sight, it came to him suddenly, that he and Leon had exchanged gifts of a sort, after all. It was hard to give them a name, but they were real enough. And the outward and visible sign of his gift to Leon was in the little bronze bull with the silvered horns that he had left on the Offering Table before the feet of Olympian Zeus. And Leon's gift to him. . . . That had been made with the Spartan's boast that it would take more than a cut foot to slow him up. He had thought at the time that it was either the harsh Spartan pride, or the truth spoken in anger. But he understood now, quite suddenly, that it had been Leon giving up his own private and inward claim to the olive crown, so that he, Amyntas, might believe that he had rightfully won it. Amyntas knew that he would never be sure of that, never in all his life. But it made no difference to the gift.

The track had begun to run downhill, and the pale dust-cloud was rising behind them. He knew that if he looked back now, there would be nothing to see.